The ultimate cooking book

jane bull

TED SMART

LONDON, NEW YORK, MUNICH,
MELBOURNE, and DELHI

DESIGN • Jane Bull
EDITORS • Penelope Arlon,
Penelope York, Julie Ferris
PHOTOGRAPHY • Andy Crawford
DESIGNERS • Claire Penny,
Laura Roberts, Sadie Thomas,
David McDonald

PUBLISHING MANAGER • Sue Leonard
MANAGING ART EDITORS • Cathy Chesson,
Rachael Foster, Clare Shedden
MANAGING EDITOR • Mary Ling
PRODUCTION • Orla Creegan,
Alison Lenane, Shivani Pandey
DTP DESIGNER • Almudena Díaz

First published in Great Britain in 2006 by
Dorling Kindersley Limited
80 Strand, London WC2R 0RL

A Penguin Company

2 4 6 8 10 9 7 5 3

This edition produced for The Book People Ltd,
Hall Wood Avenue, Haydock,
St Helens WA11 9UL

A CIP catalogue record for this book is
available from the British Library

ISBN: 978-1-4053-1924-9

Colour reproduction by
GRB Editrice S.r.l., Verona, Italy
Printed and bound by
Toppan Printing Company Ltd., China

Discover more at
www.dk.com

what's cooking

creative cooking

Basic baking

in this book..?

creative cooking

Learn some cooking basics and create delicious dishes and tantalizing treats, including pick-and-mix soup, perfect pasta, and mini mud pies.

Getting Started

Follow this advice before you begin and you will find the recipes much easier and safer. But most importantly ENJOY IT!

Safety first
Taking care in the kitchen

You should always tell an adult what you are up to in the kitchen so they can be around to help you.

⭐ Warning Star

Watch out! The kitchen can be a dangerous place unless you are careful and use tools properly. When you see this symbol it means that something is hot, sharp, or electric, and so you will need to ask an adult to give you a hand.

It's **hot!**

⭐ Ask an Adult
When you see this sign it means that you need adult help.

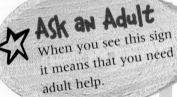

Hot ovens and steaming pans

Always wear oven gloves when you are using the oven, let hot food stand to cool, and beware of hot steam.

Electric tools

Make sure you have an adult with you when you are using electrical items. Your hands should be dry when you use them and always unplug them when finished.

It's **electric!**

Sharp knives

Watch your fingers when you slice and NEVER walk around carrying a knife.

It's **Sharp!**

Kitchen rules ok

It makes sense to keep a kitchen clean and tidy when you're cooking; so here are some tips.

Cover up Wear an apron or old shirt

Wash up Scrub your hands clean

Tidy up as you go along

All set? off you go!

weights and measures

Weigh out your ingredients before you start, that way you won't leave anything out.

weighing time

For dry ingredients use weighing scales. For liquids use a measuring jug. REMEMBER if you start a recipe using grams then stick to them. Don't mix up grams and ounces in one recipe.

WEIGHING SCALES

A Spoonful

In this book a spoonful is flat on top, not rounded. Try using a measuring spoon, they have standard sizes from a tablespoon right down to $^1/_2$ a teaspoon.

MEASURING JUG

Look out for these abbreviations in the recipes:

tbsp = tablespoon
tsp = teaspoon

MEASURING SPOONS

How much will it make?

This symbol will tell you how much the recipe will make, for example, "makes 12 cakes".

How long will it take?

When you see this little clock symbol in a recipe, it tells you how long the meal or snack will take to cook.

Food facts

Food is amazing stuff – it tastes good and is fun to play with; but the best thing about it is it keeps you alive. Your body needs different foods to keep you well and happy. Here are a few types.

Body builders

These are proteins. You can find proteins in meat, eggs, milk, cheese, and beans. They help your body to grow and make muscles strong.

Bug busters

Vitamin C is found in fruit and vegetables, especially in kiwi fruit, oranges, and lemons. Vitamin C helps your body to fight off infections like colds and flu. You should eat at least five pieces of fruit and veg a day.

Energy foods

Energy foods are called carbohydrates. You get them from pasta, rice, bread, and sugary foods. They give your body energy. So if you're running around and doing sport they will help you to go on for longer.

Treats and sweets

Sugary foods that taste really good give you short bursts of energy that don't last very long. However, even though sweets, chocolates, and sticky buns taste good, they are not good to eat all the time.

I want to grow up big and strong

your cooking kit

Ask an adult to help with sharp knives

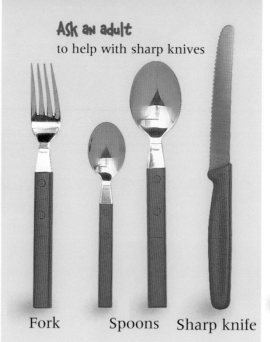

Fork   Spoons   Sharp knife

Wooden spoon   Spatula

Here are the tools used in this book

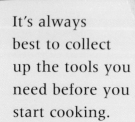

It's always best to collect up the tools you need before you start cooking.

Large mixing bowl

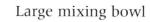

Small bowl

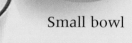

🥣 Big bowls

There is nothing trickier than having to mix too much in a small bowl. Always choose one that can fit double your mixture.

Blender

Hand blender

☆ **Ask an adult** to plug in the electrical gadgets

🥣 Electric tools

Electrical tools are very useful – they help with all of those jobs that make your arm tired. But if you don't have them it's not the end of the world, you'll just have to mix by hand!

Electric whisk

8

Rolling-pin

Pastry cutters

Sieve

Pastry brush

Chopping board

Small saucepan

Large saucepan with lid

Ask an adult to handle hot pans

20 cm (8 in) cake tin

20 cm (8 in) cake tin with loose base

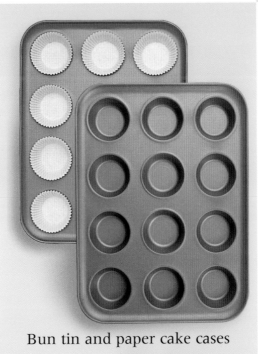

Bun tin and paper cake cases

Baking tray

Foil

Clingfilm

Cooling rack

Peeler

Play dough

Have fun with bread dough: Squeeze and shape it, watch it grow – then eat it hot from the oven.

To make your dough collect these ingredients

7 g (1 sachet) easy blend yeast

750 g (1½ lb) strong white flour

450 ml (¾ pint) warm water

1 tsp salt

2 tsp sunflower oil

Makes about 10 plain rolls

Shine up your shapes by brushing them with beaten egg

To decorate your dough

1 beaten egg

Sunflower seeds

Poppy seeds

Currants and raisins

1. Mix it all up
Put the yeast, flour, warm water, salt, and oil into a bowl and mix them together.

2. Take the mixture out
Sprinkle the worktop with flour and take the mixture out of the bowl.

3. Start kneading
To knead, press your fist hard into the dough, then turn it and do it again.

How to make play dough

Have some fun playing with your bread dough. You'll really love to squeeze it. Squish it around, roll it into shapes, then decorate it by making a whole bread family. Watch it grow and when it's baked, serve it up hot with butter. Yum!

7. Place on a greased tray
Make sure you place the shapes far apart from each other.

8. Leave them to rise
Cover the tray loosely with clingfilm and leave it in a warm place. Leave it until it's double its size – about 30 minutes.

4. Keep kneading

Knead for 10 minutes

The dough should be stretchy, not sticky.

5. Cut up the dough

Divide the dough into smaller pieces or pull off chunks to play with.

6. Have a play

Choose a design – try making faces.

★ Set the oven to
220°C/425°F/Gas mark 7

PLAY DOUGH TOOLS

MIXING BOWL

WOODEN SPOON

PASTRY BRUSH

CLINGFILM

KNIFE

BAKING TRAY

COOLING RACK

9. Brush on egg and decorate

Brush the bread with beaten egg and decorate with seeds.

11. Bake your bread

★ Bake for 10-15 minutes. The small shapes will cook quicker, so take them out sooner.

Popcorn *

Pop *pop* Pop * Have a *Pop* at making Popcorn. But keep the Pop lid on, or it'll Pop everywhere!

1 tbsp oil

60 g (2 oz) popping corn

60 g (2 oz) butter

Makes one big bowlful

Sweet or Salty

Sprinkle sugar or salt over your popcorn while it is still in the pan.

14

TOOLS FOR *Pop* POPCORN

SAUCEPAN WITH LID

WOODEN SPOON

Let the oil get really hot

1. Heat up the oil and pop in the corn

 Ask an adult to help with the very hot pan.

pop*

*pop *pop

When they stop popping, give the pan a shake.

2. Pop on the lid listen out for pops

 Cook for about a minute, or until there are no more pops.

 **Bags of flavour**

For some more exciting tastes to add to your butter popcorn:
1. Tip your popcorn into a clean plastic bag.
2. Shake in grated cheese or dried herbs.
3. Squeeze the top of the bag, shake it about, then serve it up.

Take it off the hob to cool it down

3. Turn off the heat and take a peak

You won't need any heat under the pan

4. Stir in the butter, it's ready to eat

15

Pick and Mix Soup

Make up
Try making it green or orange
smooth or chunky,
but most of

Cook this mix up for starters

😊 Makes about two big bowls or ten tiny ones

Knob of butter

Onion

Red pepper

Apple

Carrot

600 ml (1 pint) water

Stock cube

Mixed herbs

16

your own recipe
sweet or savoury,
mild or spicy –
all, make it
tasty

what did the big mug
say to the little mug?

eat up, and soon
you'll be as big as me!

17

Stir up Some Soup

Chop Chop Chop

Get souped-up to make this yummy starter. All it takes is lots and lots of chopping. Cut the vegetables into small pieces and the rest of it is simple.

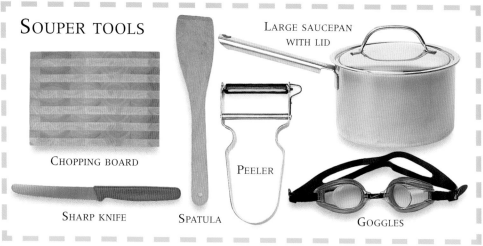

SOUPER TOOLS

CHOPPING BOARD

SHARP KNIFE

SPATULA

PEELER

LARGE SAUCEPAN WITH LID

GOGGLES

No more tears if you chop the onions with goggles on

★ **Ask an adult** to help with sharp knives

Chop off the top and the bottom, then pull off the skin

1. melt the butter
in the saucepan over a low heat.

2. Add the onions
keeping the heat low so that they don't burn.

3. Cook Slowly
for about a minute until the onions look see-through and soft.

4. Add the rest
i.e. the chopped apple, pepper, and carrot.

Slice, dice, and chop...

Keep your fingertips tucked away

The smaller the pieces, the quicker the soup will cook.

Remove the seeds, pips, pith and peel

...and they're ready for the pot

A Smooth Soup
If you don't like lumpy soup, use a blender until it is smooth. **LET THE SOUP COOL** before you start blending.

Ask an adult to help you use a blender

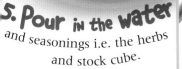

5. Pour in the water
and seasonings i.e. the herbs and stock cube.

6. Let it boil
for a minute by turning up the heat.

Cook for 30 minutes

Watch out, the steam is HOT!

7. Gently simmer
Turn the heat down and simmer for 30 minutes over a low heat.

Souper! It's ready to eat

8. Check the soup
After cooking check that everything is cooked.

Perfect pasta

★ **Ask an adult** to help with the hot water

1. Boil some water
When the water is bubbling, add the pasta.

2. Cook the pasta
Keep boiling for about 10 mins or follow instructions on the packet.

3. Drain the water away through the sieve
Rest the sieve on the saucepan. Now it's ready to serve up.

Tomato Sauce

1. Heat the oil
Peal and chop the garlic; then fry it in the saucepan.

2. Add tomatoes
★ **Ask an adult** to help as the oil will get hot.

3. Let it simmer
Add the herbs and sugar and stir. Let it simmer for 2 minutes.

Choose your pasta

125 g (4 oz) any quick cook pasta

600 ml (1 pint) water

Tomato Sauce

1 small tin of chopped tomatoes

1 tbsp olive oil

1 clove garlic

1 tsp sugar
1 tsp herbs

TOOLS FOR PASTA

SMALL SAUCEPAN FOR PASTA AND SAUCE

SIEVE

SPATULA

Quick cook pasta

Try out all sorts of shapes and sizes

Pasta
cook up a quick meal
of pasta with a tasty tomato sauce

Dish up dinner

When the sauce is ready, spoon it over the pasta and stir it up. Chop up some fresh herbs, such as basil leaves, for decoration and grate some cheese for extra taste.

Makes 2 helpings

flour
175 g (6 oz) plain flour

butter
90 g (3 oz)

water
About 6 tsp

red jam
125 g (4 oz)

Gem tarts and cheesy flans

Sweet or Savoury – these tarts can be both. A jammy teatime treat or a cheesy mini-meal. Pop them into your lunchbox as delicious snacks.

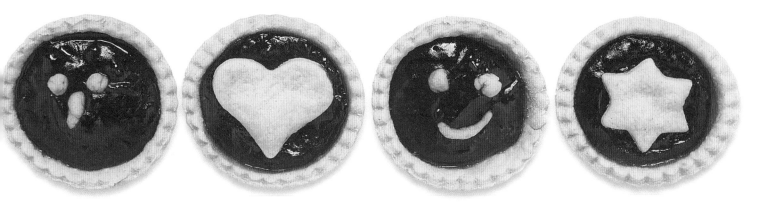

🥄 Shortcrust pastry

Once you know how to make this pastry, you'll find that you can make lots of dishes. You can make apple pies, mince pies, sausage rolls, bigger flans and quiches and much more.

a gem tart

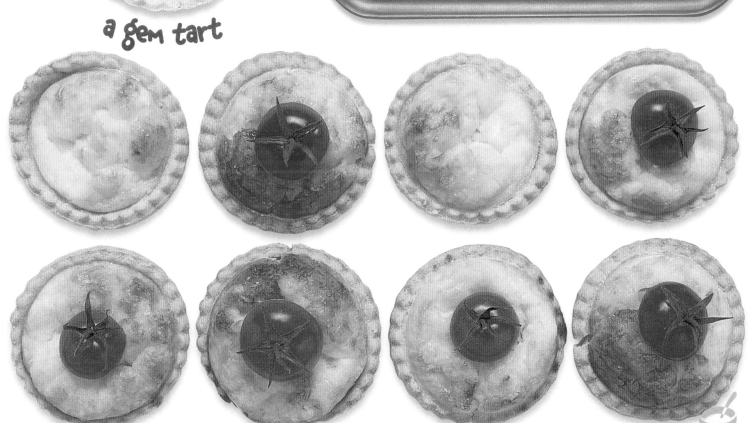

Roll out the gem tarts

when you make the Shortcrust pastry it is essential that you don't put in too much water, add a little at a time. Succeed with your tarts and you can call yourself a professional pastry chef! Experiment with fillings and test them on your family.

GEM TART TOOLS

LARGE MIXING BOWL   COOLING RACK   BUN TIN

SPOON   7.5 CM (3 IN) PASTRY CUTTER   ROLLING-PIN

Try these savoury cheese tarts

Collect up

Shortcrust pastry – the same as the gem tarts
2 eggs
60 g (2 oz) grated cheese
150 ml (^{1}/4 pint) milk

1. Prepare the pastry in the same way as for the gem tarts.
2. Beat up the eggs in a bowl. Add the grated cheese and milk.
3. Spoon the mixture into the pastry cases.
4. Bake them in the same way as the gem tarts.

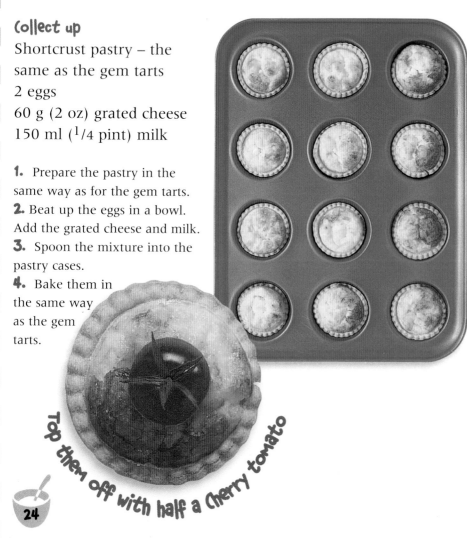

Top them off with half a cherry tomato

24

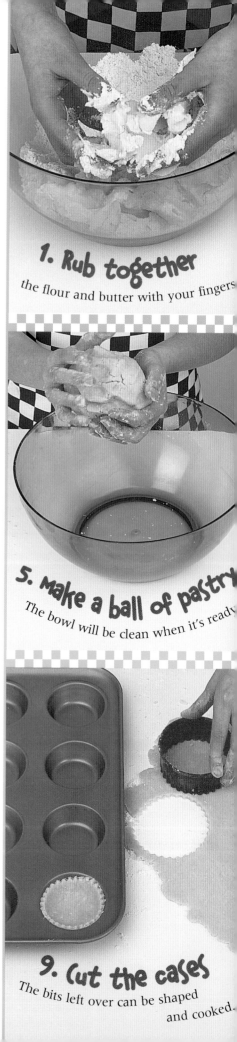

1. Rub together
the flour and butter with your fingers

5. Make a ball of pastry
The bowl will be clean when it's ready

9. Cut the cases
The bits left over can be shaped and cooked.

2. Keep rubbing
until the mixture looks like breadcrumbs.

3. Add some water
Add six teaspoons to the mixture.

4. Squeeze it
Bring the mixture together into a ball.

6. Sprinkle flour
over the ball, rolling pin, and the table.

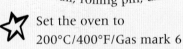
★ Set the oven to
200°C/400°F/Gas mark 6

Turn the pastry as you roll it.
Add flour to the table if it sticks.

7. Press down the ball

It should be about
4 mm (1/8 in) thick.

8. Start rolling

10. Spoon in the filling
Only half fill the cases with jam.

11. Bake the tarts
 Bake in the oven for
about 15 minutes

Royal tarts
for the queen
of hearts

Leave them to cool – if you can wait!

MOON rocks

YouR MiSSioN – to reconstruct moon rocks that are good enough to eat. Read the scientific data carefully and report back at teatime.

THiS iS what MooN rockS are MaDE of

250 g (8 oz)
self-raising flour

90 g (3 oz)
soft brown sugar

90 g (3 oz)
butter

125 g (4 oz)
raisins

One pinch
of salt.

1/2 teaspoon
mixed spice

1 egg

CollecT these SampleS together, then turn the page to receive your iNStructioNs for MooN rock coNstruction

 Makes 8-12 moon rocks

ONe SMall SteP for MaN, oNe giant heap of cake for Me!

Other Space rocks to find

Leave out the raisins and try out these other tasty rocks.

Comet cocktail

125 g (4 oz) chocolate chips

Meteor Shower

125 g (4 oz) sugar strands

Mars attack

Add 1 tsp of red food colouring at the same time as the egg.

MiSSion MOON rock

Collect up your samples and prepare your work area.

* Check the tools and follow these instructions to proceed.

* Remember captain, you must be back from a successful mission in time for tea.

GOOD LUCK.

MISSION EQUIPMENT

MIXING BOWL

FORK

BAKING TRAY

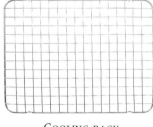

COOLING RACK

1. Throw in the butter and flour

Rub it between your fingers and thumbs until it looks like breadcrumbs.

2. Add the sugar and raisins

Mix them up evenly using your hands. Add the mixed spice as well.

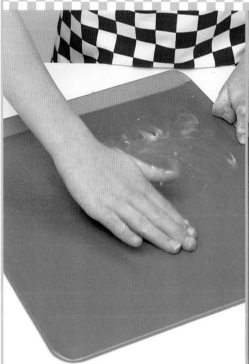

6. Grease the tray

Spread some butter over the tray.

 Set the oven to 200°C/400°F/Gas mark 6

7. Form rocky heaps

Make about 8-12 heaps, keeping them quite rough. Then put them in the oven

3. Beat the egg in a separate bowl

Then add the beaten egg to the mixture.

4. Mix it together with a fork

Make sure it is all mixed up properly.

5. Stick your hand in and squeeze

Collect up all the bits in the bowl and squeeze them together into a ball.

8. Bake them

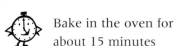

Bake in the oven for about 15 minutes

Yummy! A Successful mission, captain

Leave them to cool on a rack.

29

Mix up a mud pie

Load'em up!

Move in the trucks to collect the materials for your mud pie. This is a mix that you don't even need to bake – IT'S SO EASY!

Chocolate strands

1 chocolate bar for topping

125 g (4 oz) castor sugar

warning! Mud Pie under construction

175 g (6 oz) butter

1 tbsp cocoa powder

125 g (4 oz) mixed dried fruit

250 g (8 oz) broken biscuits

Drive up and drop on some chocolate strands

Makes about
12 slices

Check out this slice

Mixing the mud

Shovel up all of the muddy ingredients in a saucepan, pack the earth down hard into the tin, pop into the fridge, and tip it out when it's ready. Add more mud and serve.

1. Melt the butter
☆ Don't get it too hot, just melt it!

TOOLS TO MIX THE MUD

SAUCEPAN | KNIFE | WOODEN SPOON | 20 CM (8 IN) DIAMETER CAKE TIN | FOIL

Try these mini mud pies

Finish the mini-pies with some gungy mud topping and some jelly creepy-crawlies

5. Put foil in the tin

* Mix up the mud – the same way as for the big pie.
* Put some paper cake cases in a bun tin and divide the mud up equally.
* Place in the fridge to set.

wheel out those pies! Vroom Yum

 Makes about 12 mini-pies

How to make the Muddy topping

* Pour some very hot water into a bowl and place another bowl on top of it.
* Break up the chocolate and place it in the top bowl.
* Let the heat melt it.

☆ **Ask an adult** to help with the hot water

2. Add cocoa and sugar

Take the pan off the heat to do this.

3. Now add fruit and biscuits

4. Mix it all up

6. Pour in the mix

7. Press it down

8. Place it in the fridge

Leave it for about 2 hours.

The steam will melt the chocolate.

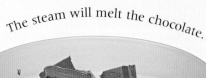

Put the bowl of chocolate on top of a bowl of hot water

1. Melt the chocolate

2. Pour it on

3. Spread it out

Rainbow cakes

Heaps of colourful rainbow cakes cover the party table. Bake little cakes and decorate them however you like. Add your own fairy cake magic!

Magic up some fairy cakes

A measure, a whisk, or the swish of a wand.

125 g (4 oz)
self-raising flour

125 g (4 oz)
butter (room
temperature)

125 g (4 oz)
castor sugar

1 tsp baking powder

2 eggs

1 tsp vanilla essence

 Makes 24 little cakes

LITTLE CAKE UTENSILS

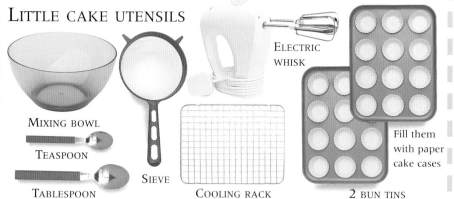

MIXING BOWL

TEASPOON

TABLESPOON

SIEVE

COOLING RACK

ELECTRIC WHISK

Fill them
with paper
cake cases

2 BUN TINS

Rainbow icing

Mix up lots of little bowls of different coloured icing.
For green icing, mix yellow and blue; for orange,
mix yellow and red. Use anything sweet to decorate
the tops, such as glacé cherries, raisins, sweets, etc.

 To ice 4 cakes

1 tbsp icing sugar
1 tsp water
1 drop food colouring

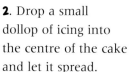

1. Stir together the water, food colouring, and icing sugar.

2. Drop a small dollop of icing into the centre of the cake and let it spread.

3. Decorate it with anything sweet, and use tubes of writing icing for extra patterns.

36

Sieving adds more air

1. Sieve the flour and baking powder

Set the oven to 190°C/375°F/Gas mark

5. Fill up the cases

Put a teaspoon of mixture in each case

Bake in the oven for 20 minutes.

2. Add everything else

Beat the eggs and throw them in with the butter, sugar, and vanilla essence.

3. Whisk until it's creamy

4. Does it drop off a spoon?

If it drops off easily in a dollop, then it's ready.

6. Take out of the oven

⭐ Ask an adult to help with the hot oven.

Shhh... cakes cooling

upside-down

Looks like a cake, but turn it over and it's a fruity pudding!

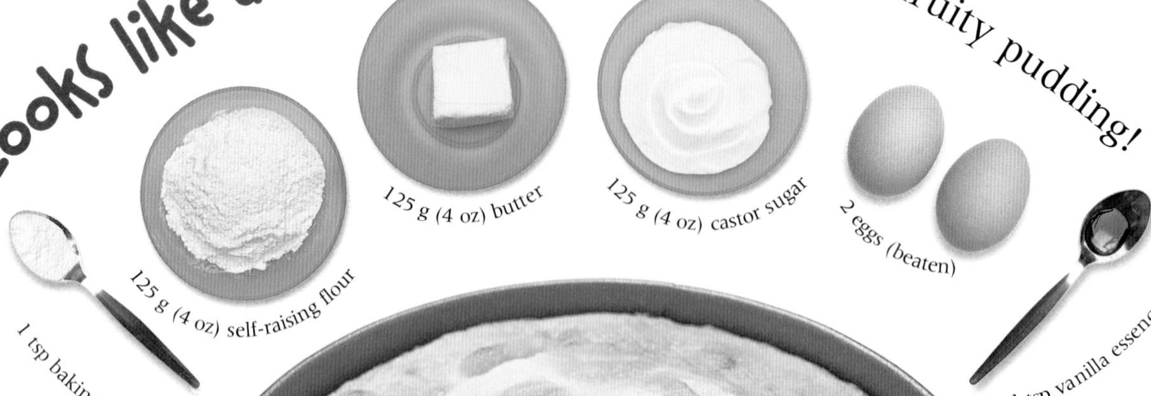

125 g (4 oz) butter

125 g (4 oz) castor sugar

2 eggs (beaten)

125 g (4 oz) self-raising flour

1 tsp baking powder

1 tsp vanilla essence

Hidden fruits to try: raisins, glacé cherries, tinned mandarin oranges, peaches, pineapple, apricots, or angelica

pudding

Mini upside-down puddings

Serve up your pudding hot and steaming with ice cream

Makes one big pudding or 24 small ones

Turn a pudding upside-down!

All you do is make the cake back to front – start with the top and end with the bottom! For mini upside-down puddings, use a bun tin with individual portions. Have fun doing it the wrong way around!

Sieve the flour

1. Put all of the cake ingredients in a bowl

Upside-down tools

ELECTRIC WHISK

LARGE MIXING BOWL

SIEVE

20 CM (8 IN) DIAMETER CAKE TIN WITH LOOSE BASE

LARGE SPOON

KNIFE

SERVING PLATE

BUN TIN FOR MINI PUDDINGS

4. Arrange the fruit

Lay the fruit face side down so the pudding looks better at the end

8. Cover with a plate

9. Now flip it over

Using oven gloves, put one hand on each side.

It's ready when it falls easily off the spoon in a dollop.

2. whisk it until it's creamy

3. Grease the tin

⭐ Set the oven to 190°C/375°F/Gas mark 5

5. Spoon on the mixture

6. Smooth it out

⭐ Put it in the oven.

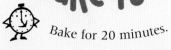

7. Bake it

Bake for 20 minutes.

10. Slide off the tin

Careful, it's hot! ⭐

Cool fruit

Eat us just the way we are,

or mix us into smooth fruit cocktails then freeze us for super cool lollies.

we're better than fast food – **we're instant**

Captain C

Vitamin C is great for helping your body to fight off colds and infections. You'll find vitamin C in all fruit and vegetables, especially when they are raw. So if you want to stay healthy then feast on fruit and gobble up your greens.

Squeeze me!

I'll add zest to anything

The big freeze
Very cool fruit lollies

Mix up your fruit drink, pour it into some lolly moulds, and pop them into the freezer. Drink any juice left over.

Banana and apple Slurp

1 banana
1 apple
450 ml (³/4 pint) milk
1 tbsp yoghurt
Prepare the fruit, whiz it up, and serve. Sweeten to taste.

Strawberries and cream

125 g (4 oz) strawberries
150 ml (¹/4 pint) milk
150 ml (¹/4 pint) cream
Prepare the fruit, blend it, and serve. Add extra sugar to sweeten it up.

Kiwi
Grape
Banana
Strawberry
Apple

Five fruit cup
Just chop up and fill a glass for an instant snack

Cream of kiwi

2 Kiwis
450 ml (³/4 pint) milk
Prepare the fruit, whiz it around, and serve. Add sugar or honey to sweeten.

How to make smooth fruit Slurps

Try out different varieties of fruit

Fresh fruit is the best if you can find it easily. If not, frozen or tinned fruit and its juice is good too. To prepare the fruit, remove the stalks and peel – you want to make your drink as smooth as possible so the less bits the better.

⭐ **Ask an adult** to help with the blender and the sharp knife.

TOOLS FOR SMOOTHING THE FRUIT

BLENDER OR HAND BLENDER ⭐

CHOPPING BOARD

SHARP KNIFE ⭐

To make a pink drink

😊 Makes 2 smooth glasses

90 g (3 oz) strawberries
1 banana
60 g (2 oz) raspberries
450 ml (3/4 pint) milk
1 scoop ice cream
Sweeten to taste

1. Prepare the fruit ⭐

2. Drop in the fruit

⭐ **Ask an adult** to help with the blender.

Inventing your own Slurp

There are so many ways to make your own, original fruit smoothies. You just have to experiment. Try adding some of these ingredients with the fruit. A good way to do it is to add a little at a time and keeping tasting. If your drink isn't sweet enough add a spoonful of sugar or honey.

Sugar or honey to sweeten

Water or fruit juice

Milk or cream – in small amounts

Your favourite flavour of ice cream

Plain or fruit yoghurt

Don't forget to squeeze me – I'm tangy

Lemon juice

3. Add the rest
Throw in the milk, ice cream, and sugar.

4. Screw the lid on tight
Whiz it up for 40 seconds.

Now pour it out and slurp away ahh... delicious

Savoury Snackpots

Vegetable sticks and your home-made breadsticks for dipping.

Hummus in a yoghurt pot is perfect for breadsticks.

Mix up some cream cheese and natural yoghurt to your taste.

Mixed nuts and dried fruit make a good titbit.

Pit-Stop Snacks

Ready Steady go!

Just like a motor car, you need filling up with fuel too! Brrrrrmmmmm.

A candy car

For a quick power boost, I go well for a short distance

Display the sweets on a plate – but don't be tempted to eat them all yourself!

Try a wheel change

Chop up some fruit and make bike pictures. Wheel in the vitamin C.

Sweet Snackpots

Cut fruit sticks and slices for dipping or eating on their own.

Mix together some cream cheese and fruit yoghurt for a fruit dip.

Fill a pot to the brim with sweets. Squeeze as many in as you can.

Pop your home-made popcorn into pots for a quick snack.

Dips and Snackpots

Pit-stop snacks are perfect for parties or just when you need to refuel – load up a pot and munch away! Eat as much of the fruit and veg as you like but put the brakes on when it comes to the sweets!

weee... ...are full of energy

A veggy racer

I'm the winner! The veggies beat the sweets!

Chequered flag Sandwich

For the beginning and end of the race, rustle up a tasty chequered flag. Take two pieces of bread, one white and one dark brown, and spread them with cream cheese. Place the white over the brown and cut into squares. Arrange them as a flag.

Cooking words – greasing a tin
* rolling out * creaming * Slicing * beating eggs

Dough
This is the word for the thick, squishy flour mixture before it is cooked. It can be bread, biscuit, or pastry dough.

Kneading
Bread dough has to be kneaded, or turned and squashed a lot, to help spread the yeast throughout the dough.

Rising dough
After kneading the dough, it is left to rise, or sit for a while. This lets the yeast react, and the dough will grow to twice its size.

Boiling
This is when the heat is turned up high and whatever is in the pan bubbles busily. Mostly you only boil for a short time then let it simmer.

Simmering
Once the mixture has boiled, you can turn the heat down and let it simmer. This means letting the liquid bubble gently and steadily.

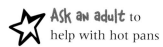

Ask an adult to help with hot pans

Breaking an egg
First tap the side of the egg hard on the rim of a bowl. Dig both of your thumbs into the hole you have made and prize the shell apart. Keep over the bowl at all times.

Beating eggs
Before adding eggs to ingredients, it's best to beat them first. Stir the eggs up very fast with a fork.

* chopping * boiling * simmering * rubbing in
* Sifting * kneading * rising

Here's a description of what they mean.

Rolling out

When you roll pastry dough, sprinkle flour on to the table and rolling pin before you start and keep sprinkling throughout to stop the dough sticking.

Chopping and Slicing

A recipe will tell you how big to chop or slice something. Always be careful when you use a knife.

Rubbing in

For biscuit, pastry, and crumble topping, the way to mix the flour and butter together is to rub them between your fingers and thumbs. Keep rubbing until the mixture looks like breadcrumbs.

Sifting

Sifting flour removes the lumps and adds air, which is good for making cakes. Gently tap the sieve against your hand to let it through.

Ask an adult to help with sharp knives

Greasing a tin

To stop food sticking to a baking tray, smear a small amout of oil or butter all over the surface with your fingers. Get it right up to the edges.

Creaming

The cakes in this book use the one-stage method where the ingredients are all put together at the start. To cream, you beat this mixture until it falls off a spoon easily.

Basic baking

Bake a batch of cherry pies, clever scones, and monkey bread, or whisk up a meringue mountain.

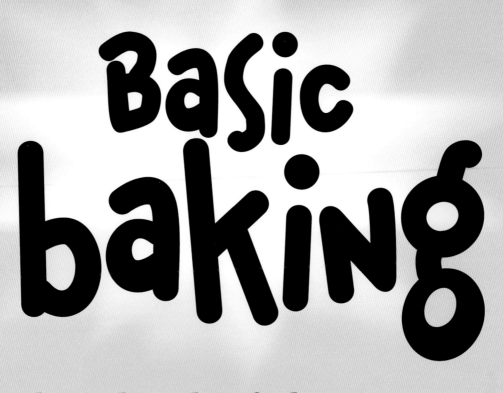

Cookie collection

To start you off

all you need are three things:

 **Plain flour** 150g (6oz) **+**  **Caster sugar** 50g (2oz) **+** **Butter** 100g (4oz) **=**  ☺ **24 cookies** plain shortbread

Mmmm They look good!

1 recipe x 10

These aren't just ordinary cookies – with a little pinch here and a spot of decoration there, you can make 10 completely different cookies. 10 cookies in one!

1

2

3

4

5

6

7

8

9

yum yum

Turn the page
to discover the
magic ingredients.

10

53

How to make Shortbread cookies

Rubbing in – This is the way you mix the flour, butter, and sugar together. Rub the mixture between your thumb and fingertips until it looks like breadcrumbs (see page 92).

COOKIE EQUIPMENT

MIXING BOWL

BAKING TRAY

FORK

COOLING RACK

1 In it all goes

Put all the ingredients into the bowl!

Flour

Sugar

Butter

2 Rub it together

Rub the mixture between your thumbs and fingertips.

Add flavours now

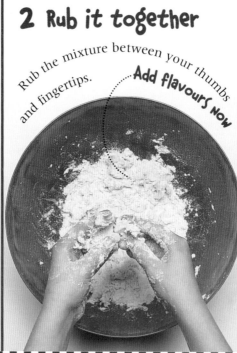

3 Make a ball

When the mixture looks crumbly, squeeze it together to make a ball of dough.

4 Roll little balls

Pinch off little lumps of dough, and roll them to the size of a ping-pong ball.

5 Squash them

Place the balls on a baking sheet, leaving room for them to spread when they cook.

Press flat with a fork

Try using your thumb instead to press them down.

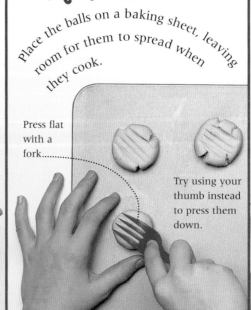

6 Bake them

Set the oven 170°C/325°F/Gas mark 3. Bake for 15-20 mins, cool on a rack.

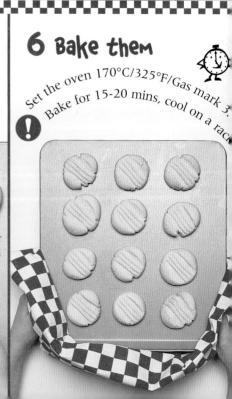

1 Chocolate chips
50g (2 oz)

2 Cocoa powder
25g (1 oz)

3 Coconut
50g (2 oz)

4 Cinnamon
1 teaspoon

5 Sweeties
Press these into the cookies
before you bake them.

Peanuts

6 Peanut butter
1 tablespoon

7 Raisins
50g (2 oz)

8 Almond essence
Add a few drops of almond essence
and stick an almond on the top.

9 Sugar strands
25g (1 oz)

10 Chopped nuts
50g (2 oz)

How to make 10 new cookies

Add your flavours at step 2.
If you want flavoured cookies, then add your cocoa, chocolate chips, coconut, or cinnamon at stage 2 when your mixture is crumbly. Decorate your cookies with the nuts or sweets just before you bake them.

Now get creative with your cookie cutters, see over the page.

create and bake

Bake me!

make more of your cookie dough – roll it out, cut out some shapes, then have fun with icing.

cookie dough
See page 54

Makes about
24 cookies

1. Roll out the dough

Sprinkle flour on your work surface and a rolling pin. Now roll out your dough until it's 5 mm (¼ in) thick, then choose your cookie cutters and get shaping!

2. Ready to bake

Grease a baking tray (see page 93) and place your shapes on it, leaving spaces between them.

Bake for 15 minutes

Preheat the oven to 170°C/325°F/ Gas mark 3

3. Cool off

Carefully remove the tray from the oven, let them cool a little on the tray, then transfer to a cooling rack.

Tip – If it is difficult to roll, cut the ball of dough in half, and roll out one half at a time.

Ice and sprinkle

Icing – Mix up some icing sugar and water with drops of food colouring.

Icing Sugar
3 tablespoons

water
3 teaspoons

Food colouring

Now add some sprinkles.

Icing mix

Put 3 tablespoons of icing sugar in a bowl, add 3 teaspoons of water, and stir it in. Add more water if the icing is too thick.

Spoon the icing over the cookies and decorate them.

Adding colour

Use a cocktail stick to add colour to the icing mix. Kee adding and stirring until it's the colour you want.

A fun-filled box of cookies

Make holes with the end of a straw. Do this before you bake the cookie.

Use a cocktail stick to make smaller features like eyes.

Cut out a shape, then use a smaller cutter to make a new shape.

Cherry pies

Fill buttery pastry pies

with sweet fillings and feed them to
your sweetheart.

Tinned
cherry pie
filling

Pastry
From page 24

+

Pie filling
200g (8oz) can

=

x 12 pies

Fruity pie fillings

When it's late summer get out
and pick your own fresh
fruit. Soft fruits, such as
blackberries, are perfect
and mix well with apple.
Alternatively you can
buy canned pie filling
or try some of these
other yummy ideas.

Makes
12 pies

Serve up your pies with a dusting of icing sugar and spoonful of custard

All kinds of pies

Apple pie

Peel and chop some eating apples and put them into a saucepan with a little sugar and a couple of tablespoons of water. Boil them until they are soft and when the mixture is cool, spoon it into pastry cases.

Mince pie

Just right for Christmas – a jar of mince meat is packed full of sultanas, peel, and raisins. Simply pop it in the pastry case.

Lemon curd pie

For a tangy taste, buy a jar of lemon curd. Spoon it straight into the cases and pop on the lid.

Red berry jam pie

Sweet strawberry or raspberry jam makes a perfect partner for the plain pastry case.

Marmalade pie

For a rich, zesty taste try using orange marmalade with thick peel.

61

Rub in and roll out

The pies are made with shortcrust pastry – it's handy for all sorts of recipes like sweet pies and tarts, and savouries, such as sausage rolls and egg flans.

Butter
125g (4oz)

+

Plain flour
250g (8oz)

+

water
4–8 teaspoons

=

Pastry
Makes about 12 pies

Rub the butter and flour together

1

2 Add some water.

3 Squeeze into a ball.

Make some pies

Make the leftovers into a ball and roll it out again.

Use the large cutter and press down firmly.

Don't press too hard. Add more flour if needed.

1 Roll out

Flour the surface and the rolling pin. Roll evenly over the pastry until it's about 5 mm (¼ inch) thick.

2 Make the pies

Gently place the pastry into the tin and fill the case with a spoonful or two of filling. Roll out more pastry and cut out the lids.

Roll out more pastry for the lid.

Gently rest the lid on top.

Don't over fill the cases, or they will overflow when cooked.

Use a straw to make a hole.

3 Ready to bake

Bake the pies. When they are ready let them cool in the tray then remove them and place on a rack.

Let them cool down before you take them out.

Leave to cool on a rack then serve up.

Preheat the oven to 170°C/325°F/ Gas mark 3

Bake for 15 minutes

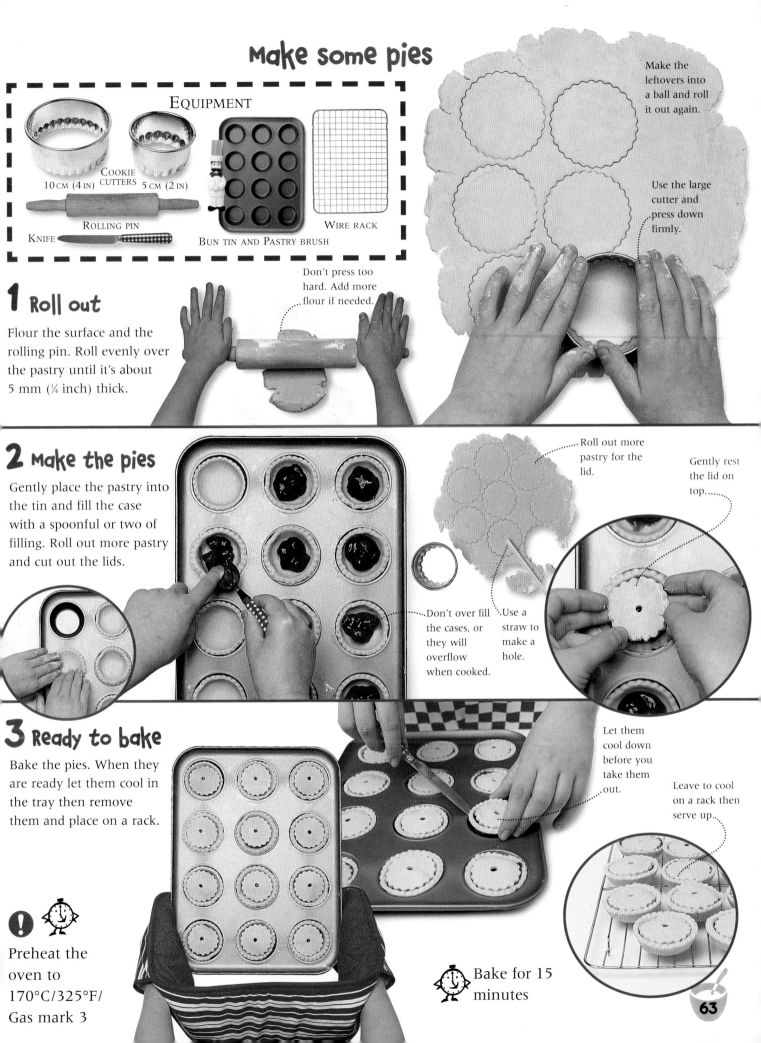

Tweetie pies

Crunchy Nuts and Seeds

aren't just for birds – they make tasty nibbles to snack on anytime, even breakfast!

Tweetie Pies

Butter
150g (6 oz)

Soft brown Sugar
100g (4 oz)

Porridge oats
225g (8 oz)

Honey
2 tablespoons

Now go nuts!

Add one of these **or** why not add them all?

Sultanas

Sesame seeds

Peanuts

Try 2 tablespoons
of each nut, seed, or fruit

Pumpkin seeds

Sunflower seeds

Coconut

Pine nuts

Chopped nuts

☺ makes 18 pies

Mix up Some Pies

Crunchy pies – The longer you bake them, the crunchier they will get, and each bite will contain a completely different crunch!

Preheat the oven to 190°C/375°F/ Gas mark 5

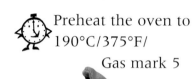

TWEETY PIE TOOLS

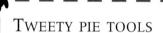

MIXING BOWL

WOODEN SPOON

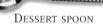

KNIFE

DESSERT SPOON

PASTRY BRUSH   BUN TIN

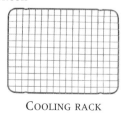

COOLING RACK

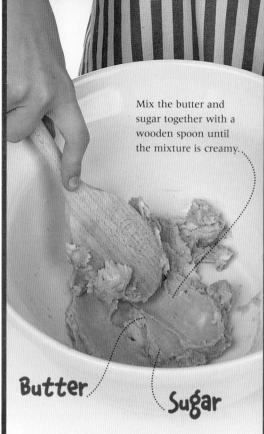

Mix the butter and sugar together with a wooden spoon until the mixture is creamy.

Butter

Sugar

1 Cream together

Give it a stir.

2 Tip in the oats

Spoon up some mixture and roll it in a ball.

5 Make the pies

Grease the tin, then put in the ball of mixture.

6 Press them down

Then give it another stir.

3 Pour in the Honey

Add as many as you like and stir them in.

4 Go nuts!

Bake in the oven for 10 to 15 minutes.

7 Into the oven **!**

Use a knife to lift them out of the tray.

They will keep in an air-tight tin for two to three weeks.

8 Leave to cool

67

Come for tea!

Fruit
Any dried fruit can be used. These are raisin scones spread with butter.

Sweet
Try these sweet scones with jam and cream.

Cheesy
These savoury scones are topped with grated cheese for an even tastier treat.

It's teatime!

Scones for tea - invite your friends round for sweet and savoury treats.

Butter
50g (2oz)

+

Self-raising flour
225g (8oz)

+

Milk
120ml (4fl oz)

=

1 plain scone

Clever scones

Use this plain scone mixture to create new recipes. Just add all sorts of ingredients from sugar, dried fruit, and seeds to olives and cheese. Make a meal of them!

 Makes 8 slices

More tea Owl? Have a scone with it.

Butter   Flour

Rub the butter and flour together to make breadcrumbs (see page 92).

1 Rub together

Add the sugar OR fruit OR cheese at this stage.

Mix the flavour in.

2 Add the flavours

3 Pour in the milk

Scones x 3

make sweet or savoury – Follow the steps the same way for all the recipes. But at step 2 choose the flavour you want and mix it in. Then bake and enjoy them fresh from the oven.

Plain Sweet

25g (1oz) Caster sugar

EQUIPMENT

MIXING BOWL   BAKING TRAY   COOLING RACK

PASTRY BRUSH   KNIFE

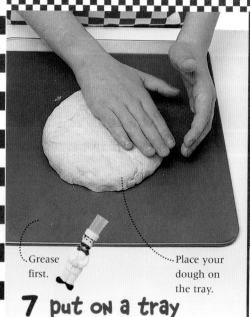

Grease first.

Place your dough on the tray.

7 put on a tray

Divide the dough up, 8 pieces works best.

8 Cut into sections

Brush with milk for a glossy finish.

9 Get ready to bake

Use a knife to stir the mixture.

Bring all the mixture together.

Flour a clean surface.

Flatten the ball to about 3 cm (1 in) thick.

Don't handle the dough too much.

4 Stir with a knife

5 Make a ball

6 Flour and flatten

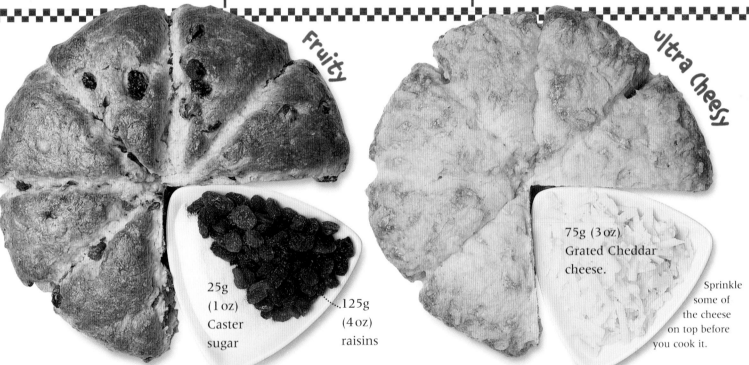

Fruity

25g (1 oz) Caster sugar

125g (4 oz) raisins

Ultra Cheesy

75g (3 oz) Grated Cheddar cheese.

Sprinkle some of the cheese on top before you cook it.

Preheat the oven to 220°C/425°/ Gas mark 7.

Bake for 25 minutes, take out of the oven, and cool on a rack.

Scone tip
Eat it on the same day as you bake it.

I like to eat it fresh from the oven.

10 All done

monkey bread

Bakes like a cake

and slices like bread. Monkey enjoys a piece for tea or a snack in his lunch box.

You'll go bananas over my yummy recipe!

Butter
100g (4oz)

Self-raising flour
225g (8oz)

Soft brown sugar
100g (4oz)

Raisins
150g (6oz)

2 eggs

Honey
2 tablespoons

3 bananas

EQUIPMENT

BOWL   LOAF TIN   COOLING RACK   PASTRY BRUSH   FORK   SPOON   WOODEN SPOON

Rub the butter and flour together until they are like breadcrumbs (see page 92).

1 Rubbing in

Add in sugar and raisins and give it a stir.

2 Add sugar and raisins

Beat the eggs, spoon out the honey, and stir them in.

3 Add eggs and honey

In a small bowl mash the bananas with a fork.

4 Mashed bananas

5 Add the bananas

6 Give it a stir

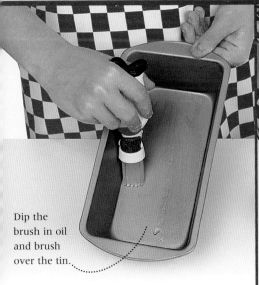

Dip the brush in oil and brush over the tin.

7 Grease the tin

Set the oven 180°C/350°F/Gas mark 4. Bake for 1 hour.

8 Pour it in

Is it cooked? Turn to page 92 to find out how to test it.

9 Leave to cool

Turn out your bread

Slide the knife between the cake and the tin.

10 Slide round a knife

Let the cake slip out of the tin.

11 Flip over the tin

The cake will cut more easily when it's cold.

12 Nearly ready to eat!

Slice up the bread and serve it up

I like mine spread with butter

Mini Monkey Muffins

To make these **yummy** muffins, use the same mixture as the monkey bread but fill a muffin tin instead.

Makes 12 mini breads

MUFFIN TIN AND PAPER CASES

Just use your Monkey bread mixture

Try these bread variations
instead of bananas...
apple and cinnamon

2 apples peeled and chopped.

125ml (5 floz) milk

1 teaspoon cinnamon

Bunny bites

Grated peel and juice of an orange

2 carrots peeled and grated

1 teaspoon mixed spice

As in step 5 on the previous page.

Preheat the oven to 180°C/350°F/ Gas mark 4

1 Stir it up

Carefully spoon in the mixture.

2 Fill up the cases

Bake them for 15 minutes.

3 Bake your breads

making variations

To make the variations go back to step 5 of monkey bread, then instead of adding the banana put in the ingredients for apple or carrot breads and mix it all up in the same way.

Carrot bunny bites

Storage

Eat them warm or keep them fresh in an airtight tin. They'll keep for about two weeks.

Mini Monkey Muffins

Apple and cinnamon

Chocolate chunk cookies

Forget shop-bought cookies, these are much tastier! Use a good quality chocolate chopped up into big chunks.

☺ Makes 12 cookies

You will need . . .

Soft brown sugar
70g (2½ oz)

Caster sugar
70g (2½ oz)

Butter
125g (4½ oz)

1 Egg

Plain flour
175g (7 oz)

Bicarbonate of Soda
1 teaspoon

Chocolate chunks
175g (7 oz)

EQUIPMENT

MIXING BOWL

SPOON

KNIFE

WOODEN SPOON

BAKING TRAY

PASTRY BRUSH

COOLING RACK

Butter

Brown and caster Sugar

Soft butter is easier to mix with the sugar.

1 Start creaming

See page 93 to beat an egg.

Preheat the oven to 190°C/375°F/Gas mark 5

2 Add beaten egg

Mix in the flour.

3 Stir in the flour

Get help to chop the chunks.

4 Add choc chunks

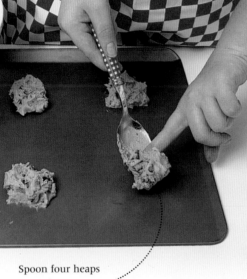

Spoon four heaps on each tray.

5 Spoon onto tray

Bake for 10–12 minutes then take out of the oven and cool on a rack.

6 Bake them

Prepare the tray for the next batch of cookies.

Let them cool before moving to a rack.

7 Cooling down

Eat them when they are still warm

Choc tip
Stick chunks of chocolate on top of the heaps before cooking.

Happy birthday Bear!
Let's have a party,
we can ask Owl to come.

Yes please!

Mmm chocolate

Bake a cake

...and celebrate with this chocolate-covered treat.
Share it with your special friends when you have a reason to say...
"Let's have a party!"

Makes 8–12 slices

How's your cake Little Ted?

All-in-one mix

Simply beat all the ingredients together in the bowl.

This recipe makes a plain sponge cake. Baking two cakes means you can layer them up and fill it with jam or fresh cream. You can also add flavour to the mixture like cocoa powder, dried fruit, or vanilla.

Flour
125g (4oz)
Self raising flour

Eggs
2 large

Butter
125g (4oz)
Softened butter

Sugar
125g (4oz)
Caster sugar

Baking powd
1 teaspoon

Bake a cake

Sponge cake

Divide the mixture evenly between two lined tins (see page 93). Spread the mixture flat so the cake rises evenly. Let them cool down before you spread on the topping. Keep the cake in a cool place and eat within two days.

Preheat the oven to 170°C/325°F/ Gas mark 3 **!**

Top and fill

Chocolate cream

Use good quality chocolate mixed with double cream. Melt the chocolate first then spoon in the cream.

Chocolate
200g (7oz)

Double cream
6 tablespoons

Prepare the tins (see page 93).

Share the mixture between the tins.

1 Fill the tins

Spread the mixture out to the sides evenly.

Bake in the oven for 20 minute **!**

2 Spread the mixture

Stir the chunks around to help them melt.

Take care, HOT water. **!**

1 Melt the chocolate

Take the bowl away from the hot water.

Stir the cream into the melted chocolate.

2 Add the cream

Make the mixture

Put all the ingredients into a bowl and whisk together for two minutes. Keep the whisk on a low setting.

EQUIPMENT

MIXING BOWL

KNIFE

SPOON

ELECTRIC WHISK

WIRE RACK

2 CAKE TINS 18 CM (7 IN)

PASTRY BRUSH

GREASEPROOF PAPER

Melting choc

To melt the chocolate, pour very hot water into a bowl. Sit another bowl on top and pop the chocolate in. The heat from the water will melt it.

Break the chocolate into chunks first.

Very hot water – don't over fill the bowl.

Take care – HOT water

Run a knife around the edge where the cake may stick to the tin.

Allow the cakes to cool down.

3 Out of the oven

Hold the rim of the tin.

Give it a bit of a tap.

Tip the cake out of the tin.

4 Remove the cakes

Carefully peel back the paper.

The cakes should be cold before the adding the topping.

5 Leave to get cold

Place the top layer on

Put two spoonfuls on the bottom layer.

Spread it over with a knife.

3 Spread the filling

Spoon on the rest of the mixture.

4 Pour on the topping

Use a knife to spread the mixture over the top and down the sides.

5 Spread it all over

81

meringue mountain

whisk up egg whites into sweet frothy peaks to make delicious desserts.

Egg whites
2 whites

+

Caster Sugar
125g (4oz)

=

Makes about
12 small peaks

See page 94 for ho
to separate an eg

Fruity nest

Spoon thick cream onto a nest and top it off with pieces of fruit.

peak sandwich

Sandwich two meringue peaks together with thick cream.

Mmmmeringue

Meringues are made from egg whites mixed with sugar baked in a very cool oven until they are crunchy on the outside and soft inside – mmmm!

Serve up your meringues with cream and fruit or just on their own.

Use a big
clean bowl.

See page 94 for
how to separate
the egg whites.

Use the whisk
at top speed.

It's ready when you can turn the
bowl upside-down over your
head without the
egg whites
sliding.

3 is it ready?

1 whisk the egg whites

2 Keep whisking

whisk up a mountain

whisking is fun – An electric whisk makes the
egg white froth up quicker than by hand, but
remember to stop it spinning before you take it out
of the bowl, or you'll cover the kitchen!

Meringue hints and tips
• Whisk the egg whites just enough – try the "over
the head" test as in step 3.
• Add the sugar a tablespoon at a time while
whisking. Keep repeating this until all the sugar is
used up.
• Grease the tray first to stop the paper slipping.

Grease the tray
then cover with
greaseproof paper.

Preheat the
oven to
140°C/275°F/
Gas mark 1

7 Spoon out some peaks

Pour in the sugar – about a tablespoon at a time.

Whisk in the sugar BUT not at full speed.

See page 92 for whisking tips.

When all the sugar is in give the mixture a final whisk.

The mixture should look glossy and stand up in peaks.

4 Add some sugar and whisk

5 Keep whisking

6 Now it's peaky

EQUIPMENT

MIXING BOWL

ELECTRIC WHISK

TEASPOON AND DESSERT SPOON

GREASEPROOF PAPER

BAKING SHEET

PASTRY BRUSH

Press the peak down with a spoon to make a nest.

Make a snowman with peaks joined together.

 Bake in the oven for 2 hours.

8 Ready to bake

Take the meringues out of the oven.

Leave them for a few hours to dry out.

9 All dried out

Bits-in bread

make bread taste more interesting by using grainy flour and sprinkles of seeds inside and out.
Bits-in bread is fun to bake and eat.

You will need:

Butter
25g (1oz)

Bits-in Flour
225g (8oz)
Strong granary
bread flour

**And a
beaten egg**
for a glossy
finish

white flour
225g (8oz)
Strong white
bread flour

yeast
1 sachet
Fast-action yeast
(2 teaspoons)

Sugar and salt
1 teaspoon
Brown sugar,
1 teaspoon Salt

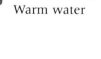

water
275ml (10fl oz)
Warm water

Makes 12
rolls

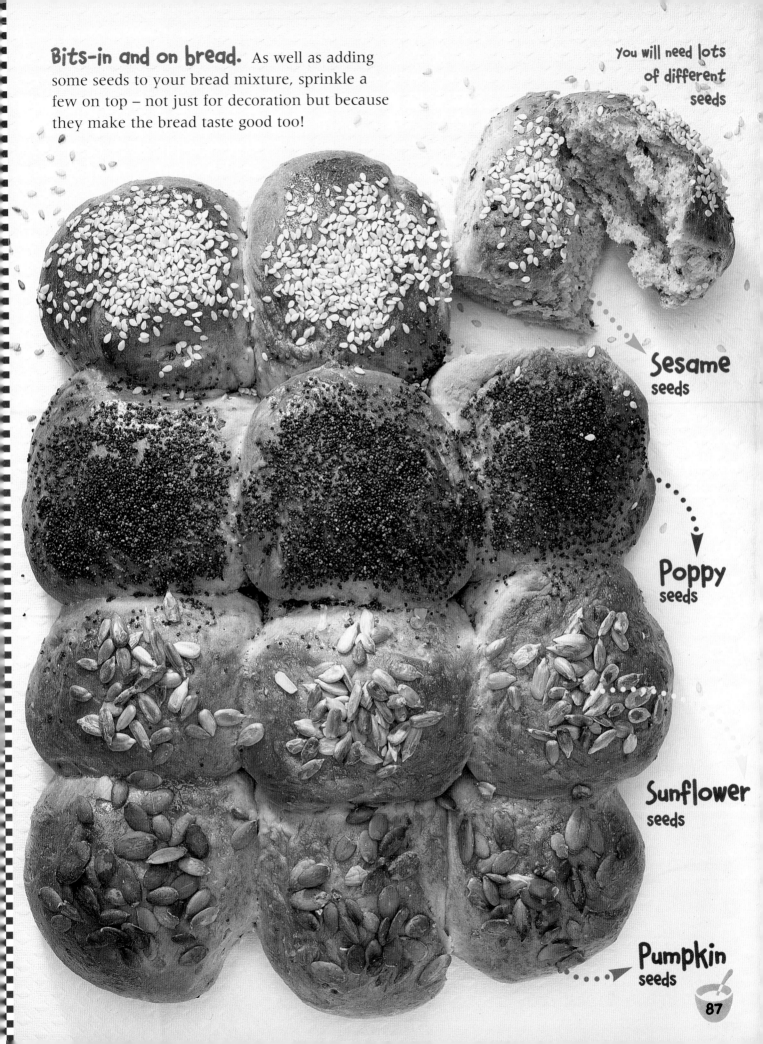

Bits-in and on bread. As well as adding some seeds to your bread mixture, sprinkle a few on top – not just for decoration but because they make the bread taste good too!

You will need lots of different seeds

Sesame seeds

Poppy seeds

Sunflower seeds

Pumpkin seeds

Put the flour, yeast, sugar, and salt in a bowl and rub in the butter.

1 Rub together

Make a dip to pour the water in.

Add some seeds now if you want more bits.

2 Add water

Mix it with a wooden spoon.

Make it a ball with your hands.

3 Mix it up

How to make bread

Bread flour – It's important to use special bread flour, called strong flour. It comes in white, wholemeal, and granary, and for this recipe it has malt grains in it too.

Bread tips

Yeast likes warmth to help it grow and this will help your bread to rise.

• If all the things you work with are warm, such as the bowl and the room, this will help.

• Make sure the water isn't too hot or this will kill the yeast and your bread won't rise.

Grease the tray.

Place the dough balls on the tray.

Cover with clingfilm and leave in a warm place for about 40 minutes.

7 Prepare the tray

A beaten egg

When they have doubled in size, they are ready to decorate.

Brush them with beaten egg.

8 The rolls have grown!

Sprinkle lots of flour on the surface. Stretch the dough and fold it over. (See page 92.)

4 Knead the dough

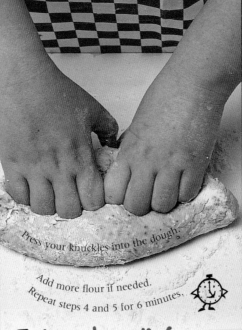

Press your knuckles into the dough. Add more flour if needed. Repeat steps 4 and 5 for 6 minutes.

5 Keep kneading

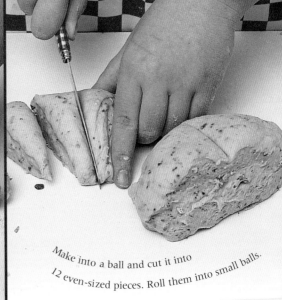

Make into a ball and cut it into 12 even-sized pieces. Roll them into small balls.

6 Divide it up

Preheat the oven to 220°C/425°F/ Gas mark 7

EQUIPMENT

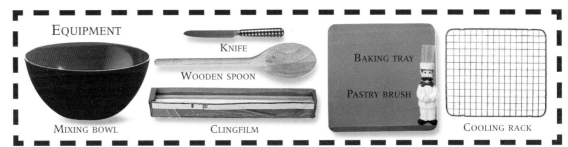

KNIFE

WOODEN SPOON

MIXING BOWL

CLINGFILM

BAKING TRAY

PASTRY BRUSH

COOLING RACK

Now sprinkle on the seeds.

Bake for 20 to 25 minutes, then take out of the oven and cool on a rack.

9 Get ready to bake

Serve up your rolls fresh from the oven with you favourite filling

Mould your dough

Now it's time to play with your dough. Make a dough ball as shown before, but before you bake it try moulding it into different shapes.

Plaited bread

Cooking the shapes

Follow the steps as for bits-in bread, place your shapes on a greased tin, cover them, and allow them to rise until they are twice the size. Then bake for 25 minutes.

Dough balls

Roll into a sausage shape, then cut and roll into dough balls.

1 Roll your dough into three sausage shapes.

or a Pizza

1 Flatten a dough ball.

2 Squeeze your dough together at one end.

3 Bring one sausage over to the middle.

Grated cheese

Chopped olives

Dough boy

Make small balls of dough and stick them to your rolls to make faces.

Repeat on the other side.

Spread a tablespoon of tomato purée on first.

Then a tablespoon of chopped tinned tomato.

2 Add some toppings, then bake in the oven.

Carry on plaiting then squash the ends together and place on the tray.

Bake all kinds of bits-in fun

Bread tastes best when it's warm from the oven.

Try serving dough balls with garlic butter.

Garlic butter

You can bake

Baking Methods

Baking recipes use different methods to mix the same ingredients to achieve different results. Whether it's biscuits, cakes, or pastry, this book uses a few of the basic methods. Here they are with explanations of what they do.

Rubbing in

Using your thumb and fingertips, rub the butter and flour together until the mixture looks like breadcrumbs. This is used for a lot of the recipes in this book such as pastry and cookies.

Creaming

This is when you mix or beat the butter and sugar together with a wooden spoon so that they make a creamy mixture. In this book it's used to start the chunky choc cookies.

Dough

Dough is a name given to the mixture that makes pastry, biscuits, scones, or bread, but they behave differently when they are cooked. Bread dough needs kneading as this has yeast in it. Other dough should be handled lightly.

Tips

Let your dough rest in the fridge for half an hour before using it.

To store your dough wrap it in plastic and put in the fridge.

Cookie and pastry dough

Kneading

This is what you do to bread dough to get the yeast working. Fold the dough over itself and press your knuckles into it. Repeat this over and over again. Then leave it in a warm place to rise.

Whisking

Whisking egg whites can be done with a hand whisk but an electric one is much faster. Don't let any egg yolk in or it won't work. Whisk at full speed until the mixture stands up in peaks.

Is it cooked?

To check if the monkey bread is cooked, put a skewer in the centre of it when it's due to come out of the oven. If the skewer comes out with some mixture on it, it's not cooked so put it back in the oven.

To keep your cookies, cakes, and tweety pies fresh, store them in an AIRTIGHT tin and they will keep for a week or two.

Greasing baking tins

This will help to stop your bakes from sticking as they cook.

Put a little oil onto a pastry brush and sweep it all over the tin.

Oil

Line a tin with paper

To make sure your bakes have no chance of sticking, line the tin with greaseproof paper. Brush the tin with oil first so that the paper sticks to it.

Hang the paper over the sides.

Use the paper to pull the cake out of the tin when the cake is cooked.

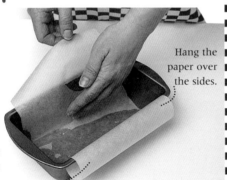

1 Draw around the base of the tin.

Greaseproof paper

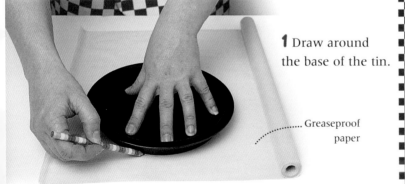

2 Cut out the shape.

3 Place the paper in the tin.

Grease the tin first.

Crack open an egg

How to get an egg out of the shell.

The secret is to be firm and gentle at the same time.

tap tap

1 Tap the egg firmly against the edge of a bowl.

2 Gently press your thumbs into the crack.

3 Pull the two shells apart and let the egg fall out.

white

yellow yolk

Beating an egg

Mixing the egg white and yolk together.

It's best to beat an egg before adding it to a recipe.

Use a fork to mix.

Move it quickly in a circular action.

Separate an egg –
the easy way

Sometimes you will only want the egg white or the yolk. So you need to separate them carefully. It takes a bit of practice so have some spare eggs in case you break the yolk.

1

Break an egg into a bowl.

Egg cup

Small clean bowl

2

Cover the yolk with an egg cup.

Push the egg cup down.

3

Hold the egg cup down very firmly and tip the bowl.

Let the white fall into another bowl.

Meringue tip

Don't get any egg yolk in the egg white or your meringues won't work.

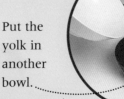

Put the yolk in another bowl.

Party treats

Make some perfect party treats, from a ghoulish feast and fishy food to jungle juice and cool drinks.

Fairy food

Sparkly stars, wands, and butterfly biscuits help to feed the fairies at your party. Little cakes, each with a candle, mean all your guests can make a wish of their own.

Table top

Try this idea for your table centrepiece. Raise your cakes by sitting them on a decorated container, and position your tasty treats into fairy rings around it.

Party bag bundle

Paper cup

Fairy cakes

Glue paper hearts to the edge of a cake board.

Stick hearts on paper cups.

Wishing wands

Bake a biscuit on a lolly stick.

Cut two slices of bread into heart shapes and remove a smaller heart from one of them. Spread jam on the solid slice, then squash the two together.

Make-a-wish cakes

Jammy hearts

Sweet wings

Flying biscuits

Butterfly biscuits

Sweet hearts

Recipes

Find out how to make these sweet cakes and biscuits by turning to pages 108–112.

Party activity table

Get your fairy guests to create beautiful butterflies, and hang them up during the party. When it's time to go home, they can fly away with them.

PAPER PLATES

Cut out lots of pink paper hearts.

FELT PENS

GLUE STICK

SCISSORS

Stick heart shapes on the plates to make a string of fluttering butterflies.

Fishy food

Serve up biscuits and snacks from big paper boats, all washed down with waves of ocean punch.

Table top

Use a big bright towel as a tablecloth, your (clean) beach buckets as containers, and a large fishbowl to serve up your punch.

Ocean punch

Icy lemonade with a few drops of blue food colouring.

Recipes

See pages 106–112 for how to make drinks, cookies, and cupcakes.

Snack boats

Make big paper boats and fill them with all sorts of snacks.

Island cupcakes

Brown sugar looks like a sandy beach.

Pick-a pot

Empty ice-cream cones

Fill with biscuits, sweets, and fruit.

Don't forget the ice lollies!

Party activity table

Get your guests to create their own fantasy jellyfish. Then hang them up while the party's on, and when it's home time they can swim off with them.

PAPER BOWL

STRING

GLUE STICK

STICKY TAPE

SCISSORS

TISSUE PAPER

Pierce the bottom of the bowl and thread the string through.

Tape the string in place.

Stick strips of paper to the bottom of your bowl.

Let's hang around at the party!

Cut out eyes and spots to glue on.

Ghoulish feast

Fill a bowl with popcorn, throw in a few jelly snakes, and add eyes and a drooling mouth. Food on sticks makes scary-looking snacks – try marshmallow eyeballs with black gumdrop pupils.

Table top

Cover your table with black plastic bin-liners, and add strips of red paper that look like bloody drips.

Stick the gruesome eyeballs on sticks.

Bowl of popcorn

Jelly snakes and liquorice sticks

Cut out ghoulish details and stick them to the bowl.

Make a blood-thirsty drink by adding red food colouring to lemonade.

Stick cut-out spider shapes on red paper cups.

Spiders and giant's eyes stare you in the face!

Creepy cupcakes

Find out how to make and decorate cupcakes and biscuits on page 108

Spooks on sticks

Ghost-shaped biscuits on a stick (see page 112)

Party pokers

Red and black sweets on a stick

Wooden skewers

Cherry tomatoes, baby sausages, red peppers, and cheese on sticks

Tape the straight end to a doorway for an upside-down spook!

Let us hang around at your party

Party activity table

Get your guests to help with the decorations by making paper ghosts. Hang these up while the party is on and when it's home time they can fly away.

ROLL OF GREASEPROOF PAPER

Cut off the top in a straight line.

Roll out a length of greaseproof paper and draw on your spook. Then cut it out.

Jungle juice

It's feeding time in the tropics – serve up cupcake creatures and tangy fruits and slurp refreshing jungle juice.

Table top

Keep it green! Lots of different shades (like a leaf-coloured cloth) will make your room look like a jungle. Any toy animals you have will fit the theme perfectly.

Decorate paper cups with flowers made from card.

Watering hole

Stir bits of fruit into green jelly to make a yummy jungle pond.

Make jungle juice by adding green food colouring to lemonade.

Cupcake creatures

Recipes

Find out how to make these cakes and biscuits on pages 108–112.

Veggie sticks

Pieces of raw vegetable on skewers can look like exotic foliage.

Nectar pools

Sweets in jelly look like delicious nectar pools.

Fruity flower

Cut out half a melon in a zig-zag shape and fill it with grapes and strawberries.

Party activity table

Ask your guests to create swirling snakes. Hang these all around while the party's on, and when it's home time they can slither away.

Place a paper plate on a piece of green paper and draw around it.

Starting from the edge, draw a non-stop swirl all the way to the centre.

Now cut your swirl from the outside to the middle. Round off the end to make the head.

Decorate the body using stickers or pieces of coloured card.

Tape a piece of string to the centre of the tail and let your snake dangle.

Party pit-stop

Wheel in the goodies – plan your party using bright warning colours like yellow, orange, and red with black.

Table top

Build up your party table by placing a decorated plate or tray on a round cake tin and displaying your food around a traffic cone. Search your room for any toy cars or trucks, and anything else with wheels that will add to the theme.

Make your own winner's flags for the top of your display.

Use a toy plastic traffic cone.

Try to find cakes that already have round swirls or are chequered.

Tool-box goodies

Decorate good bags and boxes to look like a tool kits.

Cut a strip of yellow card to fit around the rim, stick black stripes across it and wrap the strip around the plate's edge.

Wicked wheel sandwiches

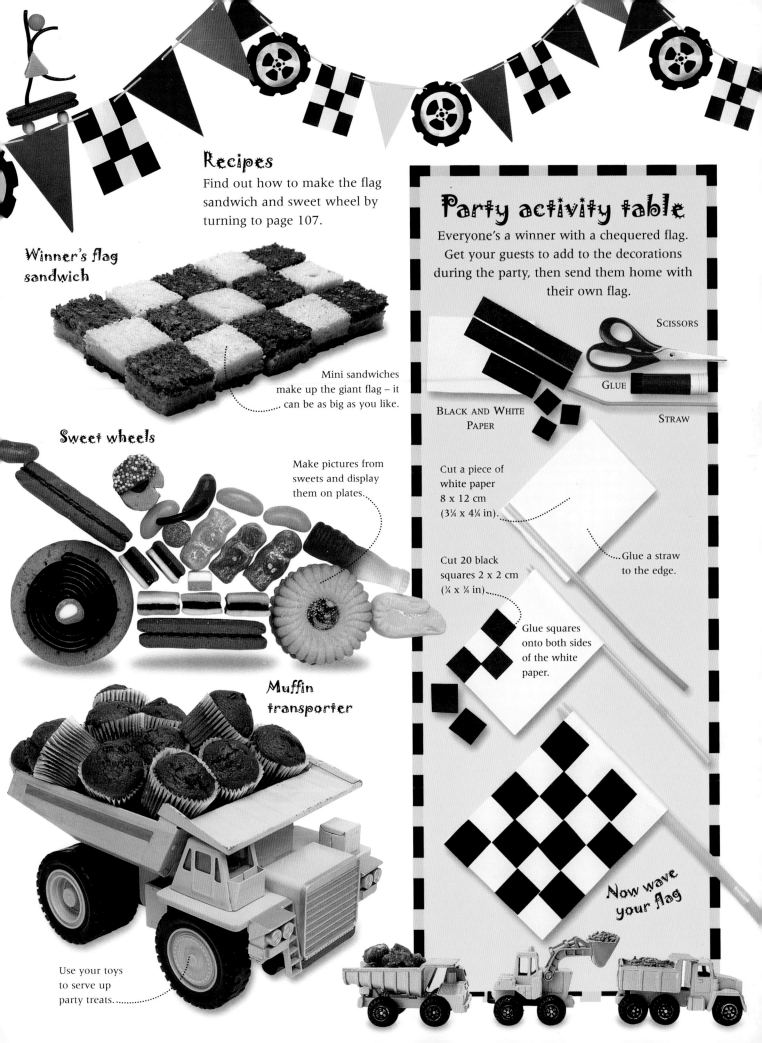

Recipes

Find out how to make the flag sandwich and sweet wheel by turning to page 107.

Winner's flag sandwich

Mini sandwiches make up the giant flag – it can be as big as you like.

Sweet wheels

Make pictures from sweets and display them on plates.

Muffin transporter

Use your toys to serve up party treats.

Party activity table

Everyone's a winner with a chequered flag. Get your guests to add to the decorations during the party, then send them home with their own flag.

SCISSORS

GLUE

STRAW

BLACK AND WHITE PAPER

Cut a piece of white paper 8 x 12 cm (3¼ x 4¼ in).

Cut 20 black squares 2 x 2 cm (¾ x ¾ in).

Glue a straw to the edge.

Glue squares onto both sides of the white paper.

Now wave your flag

Cool drinks

Colourful ice

1. Fill a jug with water.
2. Add a few drops of food colouring.
3. Mix it well.
4. Pour into an ice tray.
5. Place in the freezer overnight.

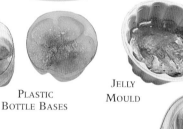

WATER

FOOD COLOURING

RUBBER GLOVE

BALLOON

Ice shapes

Use different containers such as jelly moulds or plastic bottle bases to make giant ice cubes. Or try soft moulds like rubber gloves or balloons – you'll have to tie them closed so the water won't leak out, then cut or tear them away when the ice has frozen.

PLASTIC BOTTLE BASES

JELLY MOULD

Watch your drinks change colour!

Party cups

Plain plastic or paper cups are easy to decorate. Either cut o shapes or strips from card and glue them on, or use stickers.

Swish sandwiches

Wicked wheels

Take a thin slice of light-coloured bread and cut off the crusts.

Spread it with a dark filling of your choice.

Roll the slice up tightly.

Use a sharp knife to cut it into pinwheels.

Winners flag

Take two slices of bread – one light coloured and one dark. Cut the crusts off both slices.

Spread one slice with a filling of your choice.

Place the other slice on top to make a sandwich.

Cut the sandwich into six rectangles.

Lay out the winning flag by turning over every other shape to make a chequerboard pattern.

For a bigger flag, add more shapes.

Cookies

Makes 24
small biscuits

Plain
flour
300 g (6 oz)

Butter
200 g (4 oz)

Rub all the ingredients between
your fingers and thumbs.

Castor
sugar
100 g (2 oz)

In it all goes - mix it together

Make a ball

Making cookies and cupcakes

Cookies and cupcakes make the best party food, especially for themed parties
because you can decorate them any way you like and they always taste delicious.

Cupcakes

Makes 16
cupcakes

Castor
sugar
125 g (4 oz)

Butter
125 g (4 oz)

Self-raising flour
125 g (4 oz)

Vanilla essence
few drops

Put everything in a bowl and whisk it

Baking powder
1 tsp

Set the oven to
190°C, 375°F, Gas mark 5

1 Roll out the ball

Your dough should
be about .5 cm (¼ in) thick.

Use cookie cutters
to cut out shapes.

2 Cut out the shapes

Place the
cookies on a
baking tray.

Bake them
for 15
minutes.

3 Bake the cookies

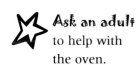

Ask an adult
to help with
the oven.

Smooth surface

When your shapes stick to the rolling
pin or the surface, they're more likely
to be damaged, so sprinkle everything
with flour before you begin.

Set the oven to
190°C, 375°F, Gas mark 5

Put a teaspoon
of mixture in
each case.

1 Fill up the paper cases

Bake the cupcakes
for 20 minutes.

2 In the oven

Leave them to cool
before decorating.

3 Let them cool

Decorate your fabulous feast

Now for the fun part. When your cookies and cakes are cool, it's time to decorate them. Turn back to the party pages to see how you would like them to look, then follow these hints and tips.

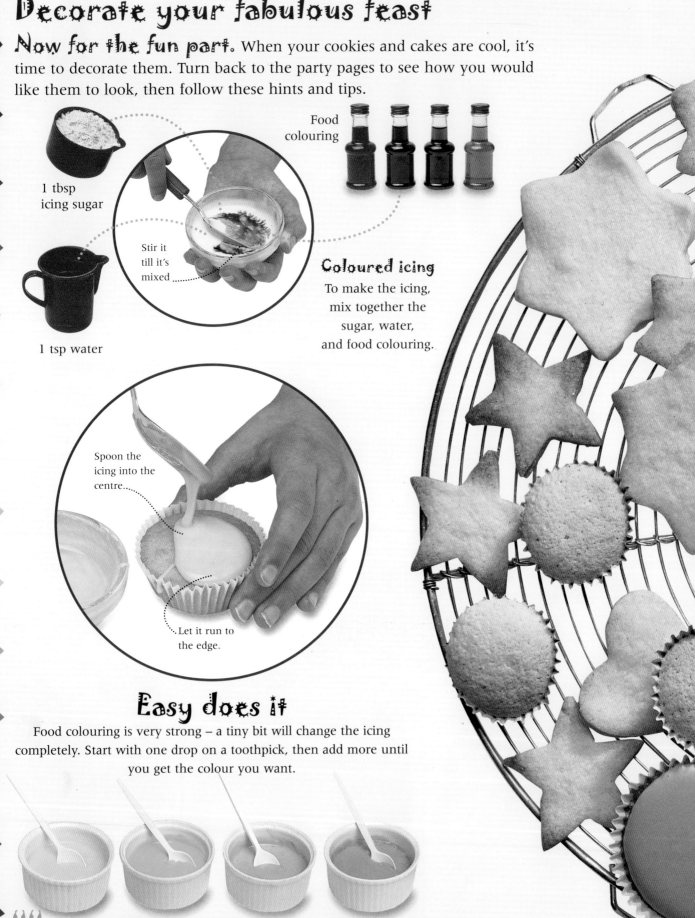

1 tbsp
icing sugar

Food
colouring

Stir it
till it's
mixed

1 tsp water

Coloured icing

To make the icing,
mix together the
sugar, water,
and food colouring.

Spoon the
icing into the
centre

Let it run to
the edge.

Easy does it

Food colouring is very strong – a tiny bit will change the icing
completely. Start with one drop on a toothpick, then add more until
you get the colour you want.

Enjoy your decorating!

Sweet decoration

Sweets are very useful for extra decoration.

Jelly sweets

Sugar strands

See page 48 to find out how to bake cookies on sticks.

Liquorice laces make good spider's legs.

Coloured sugar sweets

Icing sugar balls

Add details

Tubes of writing icing are easy to use and great for detailed decorating.

Writing icing

Your icing should be smooth and not too runny.

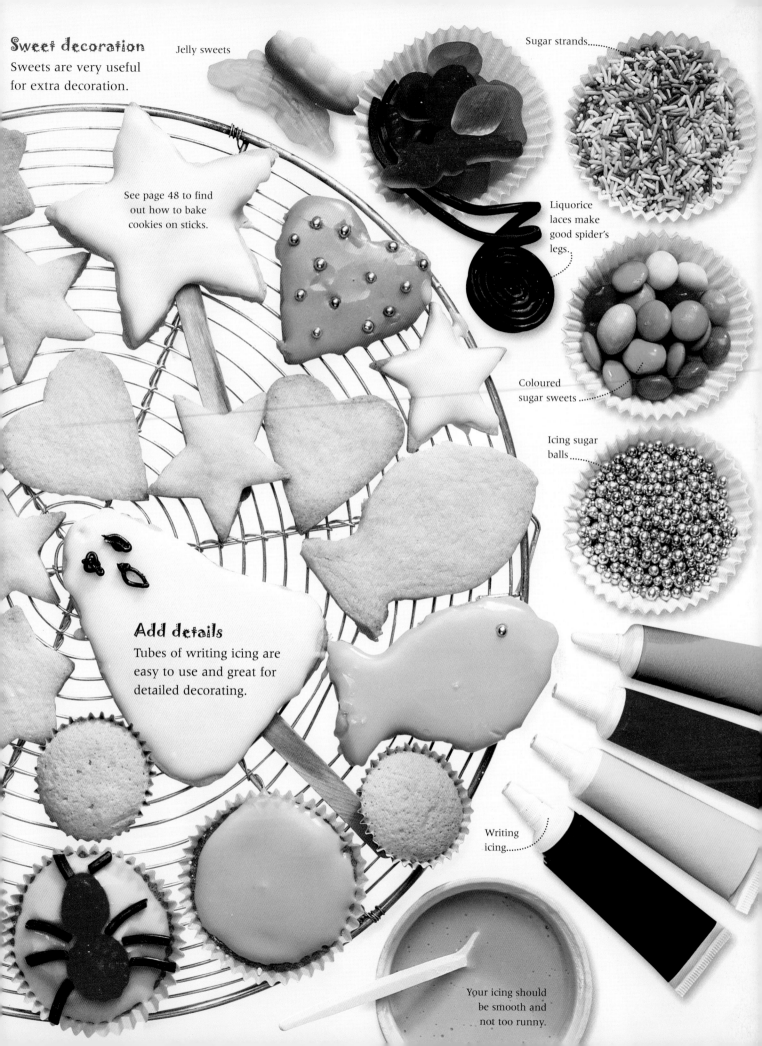

Draw your chosen shapes onto thin card and cut them out.

Place your cutouts onto rolled-out dough.

With a knife, cut around each shape carefully.

Baked lollies

Cut out two matching shapes.

Press the shapes together around the edges.

Press a lolly stick into one of them.

Place the other one on top.

TIP: Assemble your lollies on the baking tray so you don't have to move them.

Set the oven to 190C, 375F, Gas mark 5, and bake them for 20-25 minutes.

When they're cool, get decorating! (see page 110)

Spooky Snacks

Conjure up some halloween treats, including a beastly buffet and cauldron cocktails.

Beastly Buffet

You can't have any old food at a Halloween party. You need a hair-raising banquet to serve to your ravenous guests. Make sure your table is groaning with gruesome goodies and some really horrifying snacks!

Ferocious Faces

Haunted cookies

Spider's legs and eyeball snacks

Creepy cupcakes

Savoury Bites

Send your guests into howls of delight with these pizza people and bread roll monsters! Vegetables such as peppers and olives are perfect for making up features and the best thing is – they taste fantastic too!

Perfect for peckish party-goers

You can create a soulful look with these down-turned cucumber and olive eyes.

Cut some carrots into some odd, monster ear shapes.

Long green chives are perfect as spindly, monster legs!

A piece of salami makes a perfect slappy tongue!

A row of sweetcorn makes grizzly monster gnashers!

Monster Contest

There are many different monsters you can make with bread rolls. Why not hold a "monster contest" with your friends to see who can make the most unappetizing creature for your beastly banquet!

Cut a radish in half for some yucky, red eyes.

🛸 Pizza People

Decorated, ghostly pizza bases make delicious party snacks. Why not challenge your friends to try and make their own face on a pizza base?

A monster mouthful!

Cut the pizza base to make shaped pizzas.

Make sure you use your favourite toppings – you want to enjoy your beastly bites!

Devour my gruesome sausage fingers!

The tomato nails look like sharp talons on the ends of the fingers!

A tomato-flavoured dip goes perfectly with your finger buffet!

🛸 Finger Feast

Yuck! Dare your friends to chew on these gruesome nibbles! Make the fingers with a sausage and a piece of red pepper or tomato as a fingernail. Pierce them with a cocktail stick and poke them into a big squash or water-melon.

Sweet Treats

Sweet dreams!

Sweet food normally looks so mouth-watering – not these creepy cupcakes! Who would want to eat a hairy spider or an eyeball? But if your guests dare to try these terrifying titbits, they'll see how tasty they really are

Fairy Cakes

(Makes 24 cakes)

125 g (4 oz) soft margarine
125 g (4 oz) caster sugar
125 g (4 oz) self-raising flour
1 tsp baking powder
2 large eggs
1 tsp vanilla essence

Put all the ingredients into a bowl and beat with a wooden spoon until the mixture is soft and creamy.

Divide the mixture equally between the cases (about 1 tsp in each).

Cook for 18-20 minutes (190°C/375°F/Gas mark 5). Leave to cool before decorating.

Icing

325 g (11 oz) icing sugar
3 tbsp water
(or lemon/orange juice)

Add water to sieved icing sugar and mix to a soft consistency.

Tubes of writing icing – perfect for fine, delicate patterns.

Weird shaped sweets as well as jellies are great for decoration.

Look into my eyes, what can you see?

Wobbly Webs

Would you be tempted by a spider's web cupcake? Not me! But they look great on a Halloween table!

Cover the cake with icing.

Draw swirls with an icing pen.

Take a cocktail stick and gently drag lines from the centre outwards.

Bees and Bugs

Jellies are great as wobbly bodies and liquorice sticks make good spindly legs. Try your own designs with any sweets that you have handy.

Make decorative bases for your cakes out of coloured paper.

Red Eye

The eyeballs are made with a cherry and red colouring as veins!

Hanging Horrors

The beauty of making a biscuit base is that you can cut it into any biscuit shapes you want, then make a hole in them, and hang them up! But don't expect them to be hanging un-nibbled for long!

👽 Biscuit Mix

(makes 12-14 biscuits)

250 g (8 oz) plain flour
150 g (5 oz) butter
90 g (3 oz) icing sugar
grated rind of half a lemon
1 tbsp milk

Put the sieved flour, icing sugar, and butter into a bowl and rub together with your fingers to make crumbs. Add the milk and the lemon rind and knead together to make dough. Chill for 20 minutes.

Cook for 15 minutes (160°C/325°F/Gas mark 3).

When the biscuits are cooked and cooled, add some simple decoration with coloured icing using an icing pen.

Draw some ghostly shapes on a piece of cardboard and cut them out.

Roll the dough to about 1 cm thick and cut around your stamps to make the shapes.

This is the actual size that the biscuits should be. You could trace around this ghost as a guide.

Put the biscuits on a buttered baking tray.

Pierce a hole in the top of each biscuit with a cocktail stick.

◉ Hanging Up

When the spooky biscuits are ready, simply slip some thread through the hole and hang them up! They look just as good outside on branches as inside your home.

Swinging spooks as tasty titbits

Cauldron

Pumpkin-head Punch-bowl

What better way to serve delicious Halloween potions than inside a pumpkin cauldron! Carefully hollow out and carve a pumpkin, mix the Apple Jack Fruit Cup on the next page, and serve it with a ladle!

Pop the glass bowl into your punch-bowl and fill it with your perfect punch.

Cocktails

Drinks to leave you shaken and stirred

are essential for every Halloween party. The idea is to alarm your friends with slimy, frothing, or vampire-blood coloured drinks that taste as good as they look!

I dare you to try my blood-red potion!

Apple Jack
Fruit Cup

Mix this delicious fruit drink, perfect as a harvest punch, and serve it up in the pumpkin-head punch-bowl. It will serve 10 very thirsty party-goers!

Fixing the Fruit

1 litre apple juice, 1 litre lemonade
Fruit: e.g. apples, tangerines, kiwi fruit.

Mix together the apple juice and lemonade. Add the small fruit whole and slice the larger fruit into pieces. Why don't you chop the apples or kiwi fruit into rings and cut them with a star-shaped cutter?

How to Make Spooky Potions

These hair-raising potions can be made by the glass, as shown, or in large quantities for your pumpkin-head cauldron. You may need these ice techniques below.

Coloured ice

Use coloured juice or mix a few drops of food colouring into a jug of water, pour it into an ice tray, and pop it into a freezer overnight – simple but effective!

Crushed ice

To make the ice for your crushes, put some ice cubes into a bag, seal the top, and whack it hard with a rolling pin!

Hot Chocolate Bones

Make this welcoming brew to warm the bones of the "trick or treaters" on their return!

Brewing the Bones

1 tsp of cocoa powder
1 mug of milk, some sugar
marshmallows

Mix a teaspoon of cocoa with a small amount of milk to make a paste, add some sugar to your taste, pour on hot milk, and stir it. Add the marshmallows, which will melt – delicious!

Decorate a long straw or spoon with a paper skull.

Lemon and Lime Slime

Watch the amazement on your friend's faces as the drink goes greener as the ice melts!

Slurping the Slime

1 glass of lemon-lime soda
green ice cubes

Simply throw the ice cubes into the lemon-lime soda and decorate!

Hang a few creepy-crawlies from the side.

Candy Corn Crush

Try sucking this multi-coloured crush up through a straw. You'll have to suck hard! If you can't, eat it with a spoon!

Combining the Crush

Crushed ice in three colours, use orange juice, cranberry juice, and plain water ice.

Crush the three coloured ices and layer them on top of each other like a giant candy corn.

Make your own paper candy corn and stick it on to a spoon.

Vampire Broth

Mix this broth in front of your friends and watch it come alive before your eyes!

Fixing the Froth

1 glass of cola
1 scoop of vanilla ice cream

Fill a glass about two thirds full of cola, add a scoop of ice cream, and STAND BACK!

Cut out some black paper bats to swoop from your straws.

Witches Brew

Eye of newt, blood of bat, frog's tongue, and a squeeze of lemon. A brew with more than a few surprises!

Mixing the Magic

Half a cup of cranberry juice
Half a cup of lemonade
Green ice cubes
Jelly sweets

Mix the cranberry juice and lemonade together, add the ice cubes and throw in the jelly sweets as surprises!

Let a slithery, jelly snake slip over the side.

Festive feast

Make sweets and treats for
the Christmas season, including
a chocolate Santa's sleigh,
angel biscuits, and
minty snowballs.

Santa's on the Move

Jingle bells! Santa's on his way. Give him a little time to fill his sleigh with goodies and he'll be up in the sky in a flash.

⭐ **Sweet Factory**

All it takes to create Santa's chalet and sleigh are lots of goodies and lots of imagination. When you have built your sleigh, fill it up with bundles of bright sweets – don't be tempted to eat them – and display them on the Christmas table.

Sugar snow sprinkled through a paper doily provides a snowy landscape for the reindeer to visit

HOW TO BUILD SANTA'S CHALET AND SLEIGH

All you need is a piece of cardboard as the sleigh base and a milk carton for the chalet.

Sugary Glue

Mix icing sugar and water to make a sticky paste. Spread it on with a knife and press your biscuits down on top of it.

Biscuit layer glued down.

Cardboard base.

Bars of chocolate.

Chocolate mini rolls and fingers.

Cut off the bottom of the carton if it is too tall.

Paste on chocolate fingers as logs for the house.

A biscuit makes a good front to start building on.

Sticky Tip

If your roof keeps slipping down, pop the box into the fridge for a few minutes to let the icing harden.

Candy canes for speedy runners

Remember to leave enough room on the base for the runners.

A biscuit for Santa to rest his back on.

Jelly beans and hard gums are great for decoration.

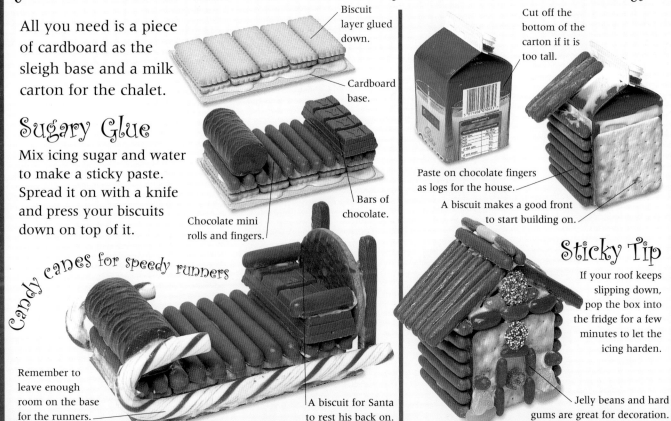

Host of Angels

Heavenly biscuits adorn the table during the Christmas feast and angelic paper plates flutter gracefully around the sparkling Christmas tree.

Angel Food

250 g (9 oz) plain flour
125 g (4 1/2 oz) butter
60 g (2 oz) caster sugar

Put all of the ingredients into a bowl and rub them together with your fingers to make crumbs. Slowly knead together to make a ball.

Cook for 10-15 mins (160°C/320°F/ Gas mark 3).

Crush boiled sweets and put them into the centre before you cook them for a stained glass look.

Roll out the pastry to about 1 cm (1/3 in) thick.

Cut a template out of card and use it to cut out the shapes.

Cut a hole in the centre of the angels.

Use cocktail sticks to make patterns.

Silver sugar balls are great for extra decoration.

Angelic Plates

Cut out the shape

Staple the skirt

Decorate the angel

Flying Angels

A host of cherubs and angels float dreamily through the sky on Christmas night. Attach a piece of string to the paper angels so that you can hang them up on branches. Let the heavenly biscuits cool and delight your family with your celestial snacks.

Santa's Sweet Factory

Yum Yum

Ho, ho, ho, Santa's been busy rustling up some tasty truffles to tickle the tastebuds.

Ask an adult ...
to melt the butter

Rudolf's Truffles

125 g (4½ oz) melted butter
250 g (9 oz) crushed digestive biscuits
4 tablespoons coconut
4 tablespoons cocoa
4 tablespoons honey

Mix all the ingredients together in the pan

Crush the biscuits in a bag

Easy Peasy

The best thing about the truffles is that once the butter has melted there's no more cooking. Ask an adult to melt the butter while you crush the biscuits. Let the pan cool before you add the rest of the ingredients.

Wash your hands ...
before you touch the mixture

Pour the mixture into a tray

Divide the mixture into squares with a knife.

Place the tray into a fridge for a few hours.

Roll the squares into balls

Magic Marzipan

To make truffle Santas, mix some drops of food colouring into a little marzipan, and squash into Santa's features. Shape some holly leaves and berries as decoration for the plate.

squeeze, roll, and squash into Santa's features

Cover your truffles with delicious decoration

Coconut, chopped nuts, cocoa, or grated chocolate – anything you can think of!

Roll the truffles and pop them into a paper case.

Sugar and spice

Spicy biscuits

With a hint of orange, dipped in sweet icing.

Yum Yum

135

Mix up some spice

Stir up the spice - these delicious biscuits can be served up straight away or can be stored in an airtight tin for a few weeks.

ASK AN ADULT to help with the oven.

Set the oven to 190°C/375°F/Gas mark 5

Sugar

Butter

Mix them together to a creamy mixture.

1 Cream together

Add all the ingredients.

Flour

Orange rind

Cinnamon

Ginger

2 Add the flavour

3 Mix it all up

Squeeze the mixture into a ball.

Wrap the ball in a plastic bag and put in the fridge for two hours.

Sprinkle some flour on the table.

Cut the ball in half.

Roll out the dough to 5 mm (¼ in) thick.

Cut out some shapes.

Make holes for ribbons with a straw.

Place the shapes on a baking tray.

Put in the oven and bake for 15 minutes.

4 Make a ball

5 Roll it out

6 Shape and bake

You will need:

170 G (6OZ) BUTTER   85 G (3OZ) BROWN SUGAR   200 G (7OZ) FLOUR   2 TEASPOONS GINGER   2 TEASPOONS CINNAMON   GRATED ORANGE RIND

7 Now decorate

Remove them from the oven and put them on a rack to cool.

Sugar and water icing

When the biscuits are cold, decorate them with icing. Mix 3 tablespoons of icing sugar and 3 teaspoons of water. Decorate with silver balls, or any other tasty decorations that you fancy.

Spoon on the icing and smooth it out.

Make a snowman biscuit

Cookie cutters

Cut two circles.   Join together.   Decorate

Sweets and treats

Tuck into minty snowballs and Rudolph chocolates all laid out on a plate, or wrap them up sweetly to give away as tasty gifts . . .
yum yum!

Chocolate Rudolphs

You will need:

HALF ALMONDS

GLACÉ CHERRIES HALVED

JELLY STRIPS

SILVER BALLS

CHOCOLATE 170 G (6 OZ)

TRAY AND GREASEPROOF PAPER

Minty snowballs

You will need:

PEPPERMINT ESSENCE

ONE EGG WHITE

340 G (12 OZ) ICING SUGAR

TRAY AND GREASEPROOF PAPER

Making sweet treats

Chocolate Rudolphs

Melt the chocolate over a bowl of hot water.

Fill the bowl with boiling water.

Ask an adult
to help with the hot water.

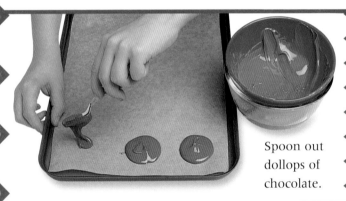

Spoon out dollops of chocolate.

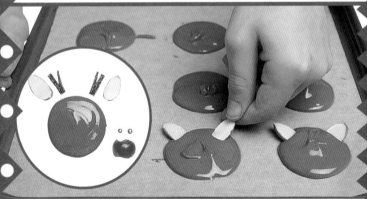

Before the chocolate sets, add Rudolph's face.

Leave them to set.

Minty snowballs

Separate an egg.

Place an eggcup over the yolk.

Press the eggcup down firmly in place

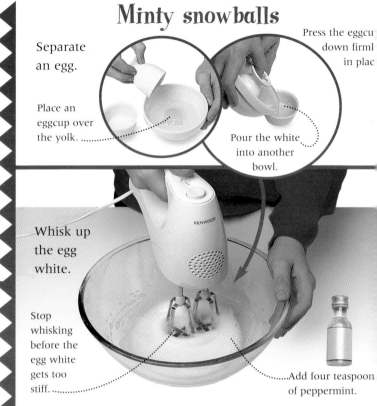

Pour the white into another bowl.

Whisk up the egg white.

Stop whisking before the egg white gets too stiff.

Add four teaspoons of peppermint.

Add the egg white to the sugar.

Mix it all together.

Make into a ball.

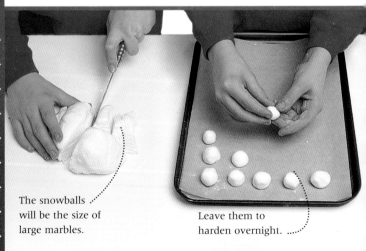

The snowballs will be the size of large marbles.

Cut up the ball.

Leave them to harden overnight.

Make some snowballs.

INdex

Acknowledgements

With thanks to…

Emma Patmore for food styling. Stephanie Spyrakis for face painting. Maisie Armah, Billy Bull, Charlotte Bull, James Bull, Elicia Edwards, Seriya Ezigwe, Daniel Ceccarelli, Lulu Coulter, Jackelyn Hansard, Josephine Hansard, Harry Holmstoel, Tex Jones, Sorcha Lyons, Kiana Smith, Kristian Revelle, and Kailen Wilcox for being models.

Additional photography: Dave King, Gary Ombler, and Steve Shott

All images © Dorling Kindersley.
For further information see **www.dkimages.com**